Nonlinear Healing

Copyright

Copyright ©, Itzi Moreno, 2023
All rights reserved. No parts of this book may be copied, distributed, or published in any form without permission from the publisher. For permissions contact: itzi.ymoreno@gmail.com
This is a work of fiction in which all events and characters in this book are completely imaginary. Any resemblance to actual people is entirely coincidental.
ISBN: [9798376831748] ebook
Cover designed by Itzi Moreno

Dedication:

I am so grateful for everything in my life and I am grateful to be able to bring this interactive poetry book to you. I dedicate this book to myself for all the healing in my life. I dedicate this book to my sisters Deysi and Wendy as well for doing this with me and giving me the space to be their big sister. One of my goals was to be able to publish a book. This just shows how amazing life is and where it takes us. This book is for everyone who is going through their healing journey. I love you.

Non-Linear Healing

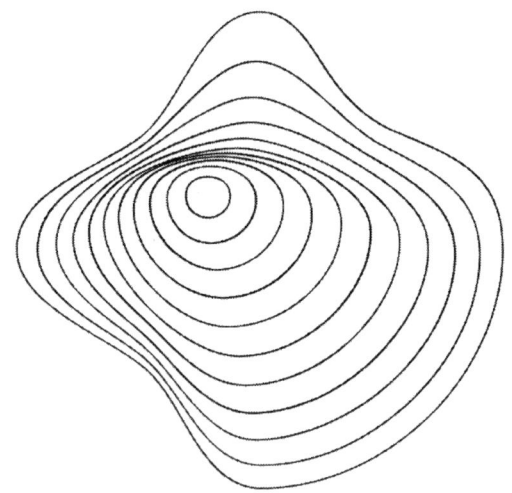

By Itzi Moreno

Nonlinear Healing

Healing is the hardest journey I have ever done.
It seems as if going through trauma
is easier than healing through it.
At the same, it's exhausting going through the same cycle over
and over again.
Why do we like pain?
Why do we like to suffer?
Why do we like to stay stuck?
It is not a comfortable feeling; healing is just as uncomfortable.
You can't be comfortable until you go through the discomfort and
every time I do the work, it is so freeing.
I would rather go through the uncomfortable healing.

Color me:

You were conditioned to be submissive your entire life, it's time to realize that not everything in your life is for you. You want different things and that's okay, go for those goals that seem and feel impossible. They are only impossible for others, not for you.

What do <u>YOU</u> want in life?

I go through an existential crisis every week.
My soul craves for more. It craves safety and stability.
It craves adventure. It craves the finest thing that earth provides;
peace.

My body and soul can't continue to hold the weight of what my ancestors expect me to be.
I want to be free. I want to be free of any responsibility that is theirs. I give them their responsibility back.
I take what is mine.
I will not continue holding on to it.
I deserve my OWN safe space, MY sacred space.
I deserve to create the life that I deserve.
I AM FREE.

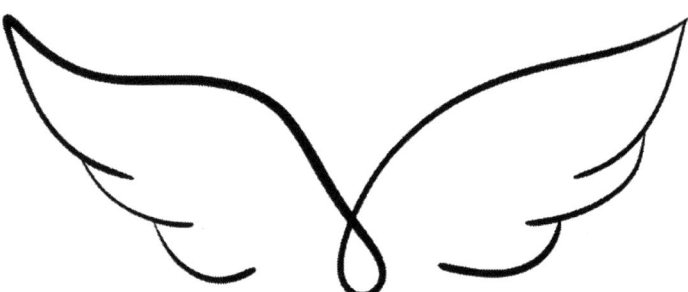

Nonlinear Healing

The matrix is just us living day to day, but once you are aware of what you want, you start to live out the life you desire in the matrix.

What routine are you tired of?

_____

_____

9

Nonlinear Healing

I am safe. I am safe. I am safe. I am safe. I am safe. I am safe.
I am safe. I am safe. I am safe. I am safe. I am safe. I am safe.
I am safe. I am safe. I am safe. I am safe. I am safe. I am safe.
I am safe. I am safe. I am safe. I am safe. I am safe. I am safe.
I am safe. I am safe. I am safe. I am safe. I am safe. I am safe.
I am safe. I am safe. I am safe. I am safe. I am safe. I am safe.
I am safe. I am safe. I am safe. I am safe. I am safe. I am safe.
I am safe. I am safe. I am safe. I am safe. I am safe. I am safe.
I am safe. I am safe. I am safe. I am safe. I am safe. I am safe.
I am safe.   I am safe.
I am safe.   I am safe.
I am safe.   I am safe.
I am safe.   I am safe.
I am safe.   I am safe.
I am safe.   I am safe.
I am safe.   I am safe.
I am safe.   I am safe.
I am safe.   I am safe.
I am safe.   I am safe.
I am safe.   I am safe.
I am safe. I am safe. I am safe. I am safe. I am safe. I am safe.
I am safe. I am safe. I am safe. I am safe. I am safe. I am safe.
I am safe. I am safe. I am safe. I am safe. I am safe. I am safe.
I am safe. I am safe. I am safe. I am safe. I am safe. I am safe.
I am safe. I am safe. I am safe. I am safe. I am safe. I am safe.
I am safe. I am safe. I am safe. I am safe. I am safe. I am safe.
I am safe. I am safe. I am safe. I am safe. I am safe. I am safe.
I am safe. I am safe. I am safe. I am safe. I am safe. I am safe.
I am safe. I am safe. I am safe. I am safe. I am safe. I am safe.

Nonlinear Healing

The universe asked me, "*What is something you greatly desire, child?*"

I don't know what I want…
Do I want money?
Do I want world peace?
Do I want love?
If I ask for me, am I being selfish?

I want *inner peace.*
I want to know *what love truly is.*
The universe said to me "*To know what love is, you need to start by looking at yourself. Stop trying to reach others for the love you greatly desire.*

It starts with you, my dear."

Nonlinear Healing

You stole from me
What I've always dreamed of
I look at others and the family they created
And envy what could have been mine
Something that was always long-awaited
My heart aches with hate and envy

If you only listened to my words
If only you cared enough
And stopped hurting me the way you did all the time
I wouldn't feel such hate and envy

Nonlinear Healing

Sometimes we lose sight of the truth because we expect something to be the way we want it to be.

Our blessings are right in front of us, we are just not grateful for what we have.

What are you grateful for?

I had the realization that no one will know how to truly love me. No matter how many lovers you have in your lifetime. The only person who knows you through thick and thin, through your darkness, through your better and worst days, is *you*.

You are your true love.

Growing up I saw my parents fight all the time.
I would tell myself, "I will not go through that."
I know that marriage is something both people have to work on, but it doesn't have to be difficult to the point that you lose yourself. During my marriage, I kept seeing my parents' relationship right in front of my eyes.
"*Something is not right*" I would say.
"*Is this normal?*"

I was going crazy, thinking this was what I deserved.
I deserved to be ridiculed.
I deserved the silent treatment.
I deserved not to be heard?

"*No*" I told myself.
I was done, the more I pushed for something different, the worse it got.
I cried, I screamed, and I gave up.
I was lost.
Then I looked up to the sky,
with a broken spirit and a broken heart,

"*Please God, show me how it gets better.*"

Why do I want to be noticed?

Look at yourself in the mirror and recognize yourself,
you are beautiful, you are perfect.
You are you.
No one else can take that.

Nonlinear Healing

I AM

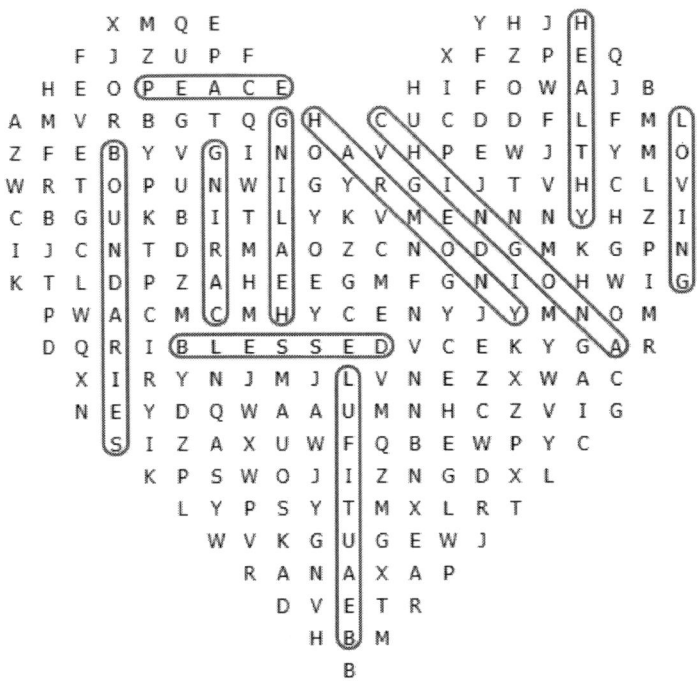

BEAUTIFUL
BLESSED
BOUNDARIES
CARING
CHINGONA
HARMONY
HEALING
HEALTHY
LOVING
PEACE

Whatever you think they say about you, let them.
You're not that person anymore to try and clarify what they say.

Fear is just a block from getting you where you're supposed to be.

Nonlinear Healing

Repeat after me:

I am worthy.
I am light,
I am love.

I AM WORTHY
I AM LIGHT
I AM LOVE

Affirm it:

_____

_____

_____

No matter the hardships that are happening in your life in this very moment. Just know that it's not forever. It is only temporary, and you will look back and think "*Wow I made it*". Take care of yourself.

Take up space. Use all the space!
Don't hide anymore because you're afraid of what others might think.
Everyone is in their own world for them to even think about what you're doing.
Even if they judge, that is a reflection of them and not you.
Do whatever the hell you want, as long as it comes from love.

Try not to hate yourself too much.
Everything is for a reason and whatever you have done, take the time to see yourself, forgive yourself, and recognize yourself.

Nonlinear Healing

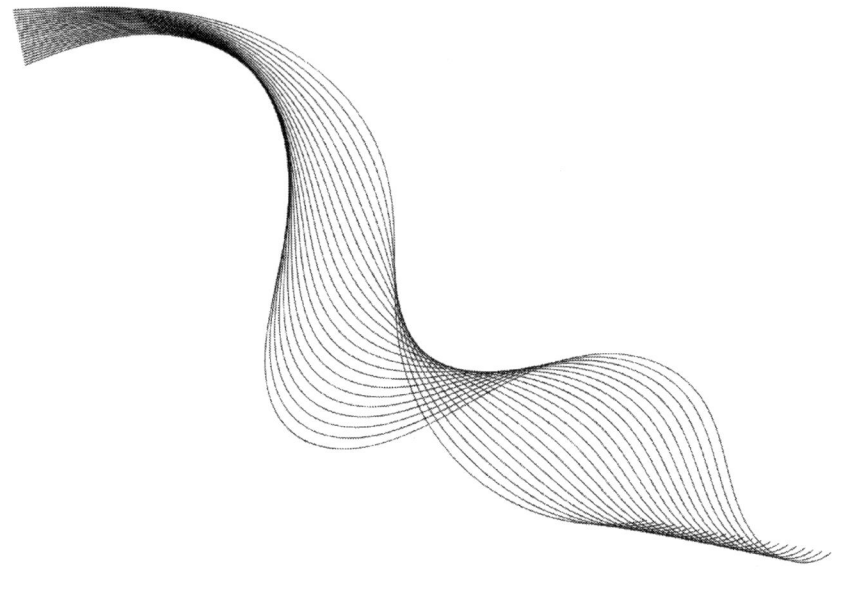

There's nothing wrong with being emotional.
There's nothing wrong with showing emotion.
They are a part of you, but they are not you.
Feel them, let them flow, and let them go.

Sometimes the people you thought were going to be a part of your life for a long time only needed your love during that time and you only needed their love for that time. It will be okay.

There isn't "fixing" yourself. It is only reprogramming everything you ever believed was true. You didn't choose your name, you didn't choose your religion but your soul did choose to be here. Now it's time to wake up and realize that you can make your own choices. You create your reality. Go for it.

Nonlinear Healing

Take it one step at a time.

Everything doesn't have to be done in one day.
Just like healing, you're not going to heal your wounds in a day after years of trauma.
Let yourself breathe the love that mother earth gives to us.
Play outside as if you were little again.
Ride a bike and use those skateboards.
Play in the rain.
Dance! Sing! Laugh!
Reconnect with that inner child that needs you so badly.
They are waiting to hear from you.

There are times when we feel we don't deserve anything nice, but we deserve the world and more.

I was always told that *"calladita te ves más bonita"*.
I look prettier staying quiet.
I felt like I was being choked every day, that I couldn't scream.
I couldn't say what I wanted to say, I couldn't express myself.

¿Quién le dice eso a una niña?
Who tells that to a little girl?
For the 28 years of my life, I would never express myself.
Anything I said or even if I defended myself,
I was talking back and being disrespectful.
I was shamed for speaking my mind.

Di lo que tienes que decir.
Say what you have to say.
SPEAK YOUR TRUTH.
The cycle ends now.

I didn't let myself feel the heartbreak. Two years of trying to "heal" and to see the "truth". Once everything was signed, I thought to myself that it was over. I do not have to deal with it anymore. I told myself I felt enough already. There is no enough. I gave my feelings a feeling. I didn't feel them. I had the awakening to let myself surrender to the emotions and let myself feel the heartbreak and the betrayal. That doesn't mean that I have to forgive them, but I can forgive myself.

I wish to hear "estoy orgullosa de ti" coming from my mom's voice. I had to accept the reality that I would probably never hear those words. I just know that she is proud, but it doesn't hurt to dream sometimes. A mother wound that she also carries within her.

BUT I can say it to myself and so should you. Repeat after me:

I am so damn proud of myself.
Estoy orgullosa/o de mi.
Si se puede y si se pudo.
I can and I did!

What we want in life is not really what we need. The Universe has better plans for us and we need to be patient.

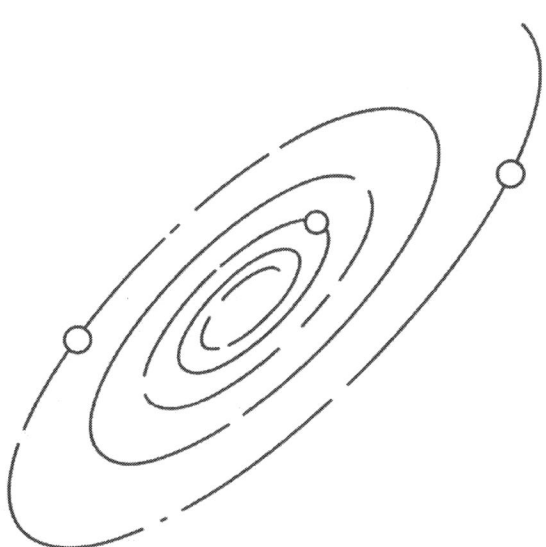

It's okay to choose you every time.

One of the secrets to life is being able to talk to your inner child and let them know that they are safe, that they are loved, and that you are doing the best you can for you to create the life you want. Once you start to realize and finally start to heal, you will see that everything is perfect. We are here to just live our life to the best that we can.

No one talks about divorce. It is and it was so fucking painful. I went through all stages of grief; I was so angry for so long. I was angry at myself for letting myself be treated like that. I spent 7 years of my life with who I thought was my soulmate and my partner for life. Only to lose myself in trying to help them control themselves with their anger.

I saw myself having kids and a house with this person. Then again, I always imagined myself living my life in an apartment as a city girl as well. Sadly, I saw it as a missed out on my 20s because I was in a marriage with someone who didn't cherish me. I was only called "pretty" and not beautiful. I was not enough for this person. I didn't feel I had any type of self-growth. I didn't feel I was worthy of love. You're not supposed to lose yourself in a marriage or even a relationship. My unhealed self did not know that. Who was there to guide me through this marriage? Who was there to give me advice? My mind gets in a whirl with the "What ifs" of life of what could have been. That chapter is over and done with.

The words that haunt me to this day are,
"If your mom went through it, you can too".
Something that I had shared in confidence only to be used against me.
My mom didn't have to go through that.
I didn't have to go through that.

No one deserves to go through any abuse.
People care and people love you.
Reach out for the help that you need.
You CAN get out.

I can truly say that I am becoming the person that my inner child needed.

Can you?

Let yourself surrender to the love of the universe.

. Dance with the movement of the wind, and let your gentle words flow like the clouds moving across the sky. Lavish yourself kindly and speak to your soul with love. You deserve an abundance of comfort.

Nonlinear Healing

One of the tremendous realizations that I had was having to accept and see my parents for who they are, and not for who I expect them to be. They were only able to give the love that they were given when they were younger. Now I see it in the eyes of love, my heart aches for them and I call to their inner child to help them heal. I shower them with the love that they truly deserve. Los amo mucho. No se donde estaria en este mundo sin mis padres. No me puedo imaginar una vida sin ellos. Me dieron lo que pudieron dar y por eso sigo adelante.

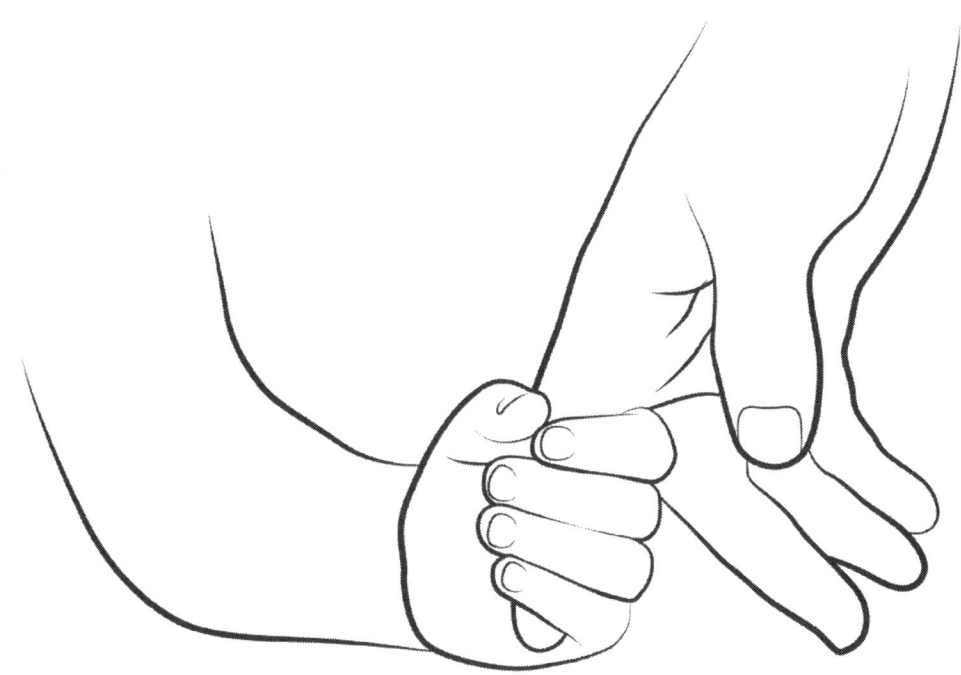

We tend to compare ourselves to someone else and their life so quickly because they have something that we have wanted for so long. We hurt ourselves by doing that. Why can't you see that you are so divine and that you have something to bring to this world?
Search for your light.
Search for that fire inside that inspires you in life.
BE the motivation for others.
BE the inspiration for others.
Show up for yourself.
Allow the Phoenix to rise.

Nonlinear Healing

I am incredibly grateful for everything in my life. Never in a million years did I think I would be where I am now. I am still figuring it out. That is what is so fucking exciting about figuring life out. I can do whatever the hell I want. I can say what I want. I can wear what I want.

When I was little, I wanted to grow up so quickly because of everything I was going through. I did enjoy a part of my childhood and I'm enjoying being an adult even more. I am seeing the beauty and the ugly of everything. I get to heal my inner child, my teenage self and my adult self. I get to be here for myself. I have done the inner work for the last 3 years. There is still work to do.

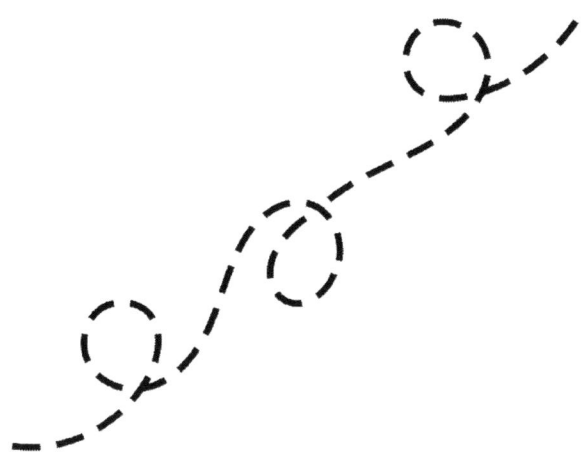

Healing is not overnight.
Healing is nonlinear.

Someone told me that spirituality is not about mandalas or colors. Spirituality is how you go about your life, how you treat others, how you treat mother nature. Spirituality is a way of life. It is the way you confront your demons. It's about who YOU are. Not just because someone knows magic that they're better than anyone else. That's just your ego. We are here to have a human experience.

Who are you really behind all those masks? Why are you so afraid to confront yourself?

Sometimes we just need to hear these words to know that we are cared for, and you are.

I love you

Authors Note

I called this book "Nonlinear Healing" because healing is like a rollercoaster. Some days it is so good. One day I'm grateful for everything that surrounds me and other days I don't want to get up from bed. Take it one day at a time. Continue to be kind to yourself. We need to get out of our head. Our life is not in our mind, our life is right in front of us. Start living. You are not alone, and I love you.

Itzi Moreno

Made in the USA
Coppell, TX
27 June 2023

18373728R00026